WHAT IS BUDDHISM?

BRIAN TAYLOR

道

UNIVERSAL OCTOPUS

Also available in Same Series:

Buddhism and Drugs
The Five Buddhist Precepts
Basic Buddhist Meditation
The Living Waters of Buddhism
Basic Buddhism for a World in Trouble
Dependent Origination (*Paṭiccasamuppāda*)
The Ten Fetters (*Saŋyojana*)
Buddhist Pali Chants (with English Translations)
The Five Nivāraṇas (*Buddha's Teaching of the Five Hindrances*)

Published by Universal Octopus 2018
universaloctopus.com

ISBN 978-1-9999063-5-1

WHAT IS BUDDHISM?

Buddhism is a method by which one can put an end to the suffering that we experience in this world.

'Suffering' means all those experiences, large and small, which have characteristics that we do not want. Experiences that are painful, unpleasant, tiresome, frustrating, irritating or depressing.

Birth is suffering. Sickness is suffering. Old age is suffering. Death is suffering. Not having what we want is suffering. Having to put up with what we do not want is suffering.

Suffering is experienced through the six sense doors. Bodily suffering is felt when the sense of touch comes into contact with a disagreeable sense object, something hot or sharp or pressing. It also occurs when the more sensitive organs of touch - the eye, the ear, the nose and the tongue - come into contact with stimuli to which they are vulnerable. The eye is affected by light, the ear by sound waves, the nose by gases and particles, and the tongue by objects of taste.

The mind organ also experiences suffering by way of states of mind and thoughts: regret, remorse, anger, envy, worry, restlessness, jealousy, despair, loneliness, desire.

Apart from these six senses, no suffering is experienced, since it is through the senses that sense objects are contacted and experience takes place.

Without these senses there would be no experience at all and no suffering.

Without our senses, the world would not exist for us.

According to Buddhism, things occur because there is a cause for them: a footprint needs a foot; warmth requires a source of heat and so on. Few would deny this, but in Buddhism it is taken further and applied universally. Death occurs because there is Birth. Birth occurs because there is a desire to be born.

Suffering, too, does not occur spontaneously. It also has a cause. The cause of suffering is the grasping out through the six senses at the objects of sense and the clinging to them. If we did not do this we would not suffer.

Consider the analogy of the red-hot poker. If we grasp after it and cling to it, our hand is burned and we suffer.

Conversely, if the cause is removed, then the effect will cease. No foot, no footprint. No birth, no death. If we let go of the poker and no longer grasp after it, our wounds will heal in due course and after that there will be no more pain.

Why does one grasp out through the six senses at the sense objects that make up the experiences of life?

Because one considers them desirable.

One wants to be born. One wants the poker. This strong desire clouds one's judgement so that one is unable to see the other side; the consequences.

Being born means sickness, old age and death. Grasping the poker means being burned.

Buddhism attempts to tell us (or remind us) that the state of *not* grasping out through the senses at sense objects is an absolute, eternal state of pure peace and happiness. It calls this Nibbāna[1].

It is not death, as those who believe there is only one life understand death. They see it as the destruction of something that exists.

Nibbāna is like a cinema screen. The universe is all the pictures and images superimposed upon that screen.

Because of the pictures, we can't see the screen. Yet it is there all the time. If we could, all at once, remove all the pictures from the screen, we would see it immediately.

All the pictures, which succeed each other so rapidly, are none of them real; the fire is not hot, the water is not wet, the heroine is not a real girl.

---

[1] *See NOTES page 19*

Becoming disenchanted with the illusion of it all, suddenly one sees the screen behind it. Similarly, when one becomes disenchanted with the endless flow of phenomena at the sense doors, one has a sudden, direct experience of Nibbāna.

Or, if <u>we</u> could make the effort to <u>stop</u> all sense perceptions, feelings, thoughts and images, Nibbāna would be revealed.

When (if) we find the whole universe, mind and body, unsatisfactory, and let it go, it falls away from us and we experience total Peace and Happiness.

This is a state that has always been there. From time to time we get flashes of it. It is not death. Death is the end of something.

Nibbāna is not the end of anything. It is a state without a beginning and without an end.

This is the Buddha's analysis, called the "Noble Truths", of how things actually <u>are</u> in our world and our lives. Plus he indicates the cause and the solution. Buddhism also reveals a <u>method</u> for achieving the solution.

It is a way of behaving and acting in everyday life, which is designed to help human beings tread the **Path**, step by step, to a personal realisation of the state of Nibbāna.

The Path to Freedom from Suffering.

The Eightfold Path:

> **Right Seeing/View**
> (sammā-ditthi)
>
> **Right Thought/Intention**
> (sammā-sankappa)
>
> **Right Speech**
> (sammā-vācā)
>
> **Right Action**
> (sammā-kammanta)
>
> **Right Livelihood**
> (sammā-ājīva)
>
> **Right Effort**
> (sammā-vāyāma)
>
> **Right Mindfulness**
> (sammā-sati)
>
> **Right Concentration**
> (sammā-samādhi)

But all eight need to be developed simultaneously and not one after another. Seeing the individual headings as spokes of the Dharma Wheel rather than as a list indicates their inter-relatedness.

Buddhism is practical, not theoretical.

By personal experience, the Buddha discovered the truth about the origin of suffering. He then discovered, and experienced for himself, during his lifetime, how to put a stop to suffering.

Finally, he communicated this method by which other serious men could follow in his footsteps, see the truth for themselves and attain the same goal.

It is a restructuring of one's lifestyle, starting in the mind and covering all activities of thought, word and deed.

Those areas in a man's life have been identified which may need to change and develop if he wants to reach the goal in the most efficient way.

An athlete doesn't develop his muscles individually. He develops his whole body as he goes along, giving more or less attention to those areas that need it. These may very well vary with time.

However, obviously <u>viewpoint</u> will be a determining factor which <u>will</u> affect all the others.

The butcher's view is that it is acceptable to provide dead animals for humans to eat. Others will have different views. Which is "right view"?

So, initially, **Right View** requires the most attention. Then, it can be applied to the other aspects of a man's life so that he can progress in harmony both within himself and with others.

The Buddha introduced this method over 2,500 years ago and it still exists in its original form. Even today, men and women, who conscientiously put it into actual practice, are able to put an end to suffering and reach Nibbāna.

PRELIMINARY

The emphasis in Buddhism has always been on identifying the **cause** of suffering. The practice of Buddhism starts therefore with an acceptance of the **Five Precepts**.

These are undertakings not to **cause** suffering for oneself and others and to abstain from all actions which cause suffering:-

> **Killing**
> **Stealing**
> **Misuse of the Senses**[2]
> **Lying**
> **Drinks and Drugs which lead to carelessness**

---

[2] *Misuse of the Senses. See NOTES page 19*

It is obvious that if one sticks to the spirit and letter of these, one will eliminate serious ways in which one is a cause of suffering to others and oneself.

By doing this, one takes a stand against Suffering and this enables one to see it more clearly as it appears in day-to-day life, especially in the world around us.

One's conscience clears and the more immediate problems in everyday life subside, leaving one more peaceful and clear-sighted.

The three activities that make up one's life – thought, speech and actions – become apparent. One is in a position to adopt in earnest a detailed method of practice which provides the most efficient and direct route to Nibbāna.

Right View: Is primarily concerned with actually seeing the universality of suffering and the impossibility of finally escaping from it while one still wants those things that lead to suffering. The most obvious of these is Birth itself. No Birth, no Death. No Suffering in between.

It also involves seeing that things do not happen chaotically or by chance but by cause and effect. If this, then that.

More importantly; *if not this, then not that.* If you can choose to take charge of the causes, you can control the effects.

It is particularly relevant in the realm of birth and rebirth, where there is an overflow from the one to the other.

This leads us to the very heart of Ethics.

I don't do to other living beings things that cause suffering and which I would not want done to myself.

The Law is mirror-like in its precision
and its simplicity needs no revision;
that Good breeds Good
and Evil has its price;
that Virtue is its own reward.
And so is Vice.

Right Thought: Is thought free from sensuous desire, from ill will and cruelty.

Right Speech: Abstaining from lying, tale bearing, harsh language and foolish speech.

Right (Bodily) Action: Abstaining from killing, stealing and misuse of the senses (including sexual misconduct).

Right Livelihood: Abstaining from a livelihood that causes harm to other living beings, such as trading in arms, in living beings, intoxicating drinks and fishing. Or working as a soldier. Or is deceitful, treacherous and involves trickery. Or fortune telling and usury etc.

Right Effort: The effort to avoid or overcome evil and unwholesome things, and the effort to develop and maintain good and wholesome things.

Right Mindfulness: Mindfulness and awareness, from moment to moment, in contemplating body, feelings, mind and mind-objects.

Right Concentration: The term 'Samadhi' derives from the Sanskrit root *sam-a-dha*; *sam* (together) + *a* (toward) + *dadhati* (put). Hence, it means "putting together, collecting".

It is often translated as 'concentration' in English.

This is not entirely wrong but it does not go deep enough or reveal the significance of the word in Buddhism and Hinduism. It is also associated with the term Samatha (abiding calm). In the suttas, Samadhi is defined as one-pointedness of mind *(cittass'ekaggatā)*.

'Samadhi' in Buddhism is calming the mind and its 'formations'. This is done by practising single-pointed meditation, most commonly through mindfulness of breathing. Or, by concentration on a meditation-object.

With the development of Samatha (abiding calm), one is in a position to suppress, and ultimately put an end to, the obscuring hindrances:

Sensual desire
Ill-will
Sloth and Torpor
Restlessness and Regret
and Doubt

With the suppression of these hindrances, calm meditation progresses and leads to *Pīti,* a feeling of joy, gladness and rapture, and detachment.

Further perseverance and refinement of the practice leads to a prolonged deepening of this state of calm and, ultimately, to the experience of Nibbāna in this very life.

Together with the experience, comes understanding of its significance.

This enables one to complete the purification process and prolong it indefinitely, both within and beyond this lifetime.

This is the practice of Buddhist Meditation. The mind is calmed and controlled and becomes a useful tool instead of a bad master. We can investigate our lives, the origins of our lives and how we have become trapped in an on-going world of suffering.

It enables us to break free from our fetters and reach Happiness and Peace.

Details of this practice are discussed in

Basic Buddhist Meditation.

NOTES

1. **Nibbāna/Nirvāna** *(See page 8):*
The original Sanskrit root is *nis:* "without, outside" + *vāna (*past participle of *vā):* "to blow".

This is often understood in the sense of *blown out,* which involves the notion of *heat.* When the fires of craving and desire have *blown out.*

But it can also, and significantly, be seen as *without blowing.* When there is no blower and no blowing, and the blowing has stopped, the original state of stillness and calm is revealed.

This is much more relevant to the mind. (Heated mind-states are got rid of long before the ripples of thought are abandoned.)

2. **"Misuse of the Senses"** *(See page 13):*
   The Third Precept:

> *"I undertake to observe the precept to abstain from misuse of the senses."*

**KĀMESU MICCHĀCĀRĀ VERAMAṆĪ
SIKKHĀPADAṀ SAMĀDIYĀMI.**

KĀMESU MICCHĀCĀRĀ literally and originally means: *misuse of the senses.* That is, of <u>any</u> of the senses. Later, and especially recently, it has acquired the more limited meaning of "sexual misconduct", which is obviously variously interpreted by different cultures and in different places.

Misleadingly, this has acquired the status of a Standard English translation.

Of course, it <u>does</u> include sexual misconduct, especially for lay people. Monks, after all, are not supposed to engage in any sexual activity.

In reality, all five senses originally came into existence as windows on the world, through which we gather information to assist survival and avoid non-survival.

That dog bites, avoid it!
That snake's bite kills. Be careful!
That food tastes good: I can eat it!
That one tastes rotten. Try another!
That smells alright; taste it!
That smells decaying, unhealthy. No!
That feels too hot; steer clear!
That's sharp, piercing. Painful!

Because of misuse, the senses have become, for humans, portals for desire and dislike, and, with the advent of the Ego, entry points for craving and aversion, the source of all our troubles.

Through our eyes, we feed our minds with pornographic films and books to provide more misguided sensual stimulation of the same kind.

Through our ears, we listen to gossip and misinformation, seek flattery and avoid unwelcome truths.

With our noses and tongues we seek titillation and indulgence, become obese and malnourished.

And, all the while, our minds (and our world) become a refuse heap which seeks increasing impurities through these senses.

So, yes, misuse of <u>any</u> of the senses. Especially, the mind!

THE QUIET MIND

The Sun shines
in a bucket of water
and doesn't
get
wet.